TABLE OF CONTI

SYMBOLS AND SIGNS

PROCEDURES

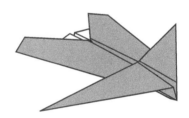

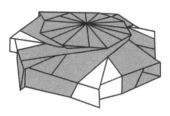

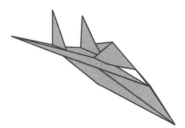

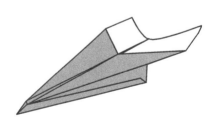

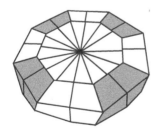

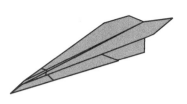

Hex
page 28

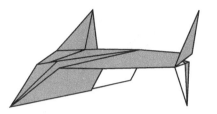

Aeon
page 32

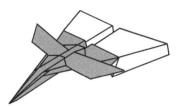

Sundown
page 36

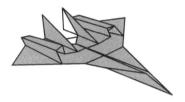

Razorback
page 41

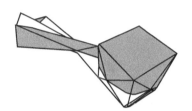

Hammer
page 46

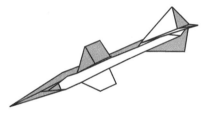

Longsword
page 51

Dark Knight
page 55

Mourningstar
page 60

EASY AIRCRAFT ORIGAMI

14 Cool Paper Projects Take Flight

JAYSON MERRILL

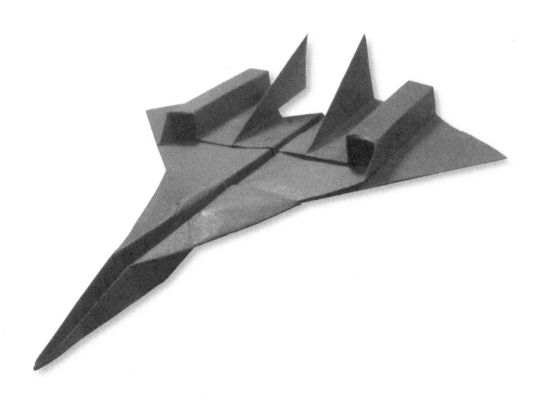

DOVER PUBLICATIONS, INC.

Mineola, New York

INTRODUCTION

This book will instruct you on how to fold 14 unique models. With these projects, I wish to broaden the amount of models for beginners to fold. They go beyond just darts and gliders and go into more creative directions. I want to inspire folders to continue folding and creating new and different types of aircraft. Most of the models are simple but some are for slightly more experienced folders. Feel free to experiment and push the limits of what can fly.

Bibliographical Note

Easy Aircraft Origami: 14 Cool Paper Projects Take Flight is a new work,
first published by Dover Publications, Inc., in 2020.

Library of Congress Cataloging-in-Publication Data

Names: Merrill, Jayson, author.
Title: Easy aircraft origami: 14 cool paper projects take flight / Jayson Merrill.
Description: Mineola, New York: Dover Publications, Inc., 2020.
Identifiers: LCCN 2019060261 | ISBN 9780486841250 (paperback) | ISBN 0486841251
  (paperback)
Subjects: LCSH: Origami. | Paper airplanes.
Classification: LCC TT872.5 .M4695 2020 | DDC 736/.982—dc23
LC record available at https://lccn.loc.gov/2019060261

Manufactured in the United States by LSC Communications
84125101
www.doverpublications.com

2 4 6 8 10 9 7 5 3 1

2020

SYMBOLS AND SIGNS

Lines

——————————— This line indicates an edge.

··························· This line indicates a hidden edge.

- - - - - - - - - - - This line indicates where to make a valley fold.

- · - · - · - · - · - · · This lines indicates where to make a mountain fold.

···································· This lines indicates a hidden fold.

Arrows

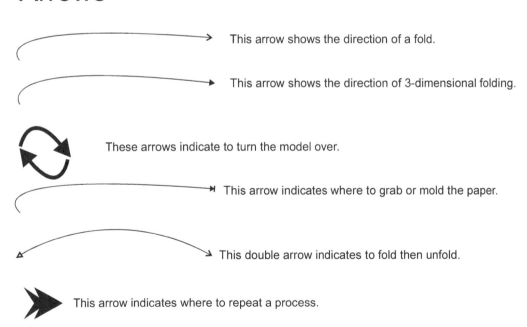

This arrow shows the direction of a fold.

This arrow shows the direction of 3-dimensional folding.

These arrows indicate to turn the model over.

This arrow indicates where to grab or mold the paper.

This double arrow indicates to fold then unfold.

This arrow indicates where to repeat a process.

PROCEDURES

Inside reverse fold

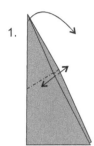

1.

2.

Partially open the sides out and push the top in.

Outside reverse fold

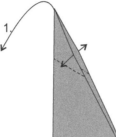

1.

2.

Partially open the sides out and push the top backward.

Squash fold

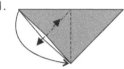

1.

2.

Pull the sides apart and push the corner down.

Rabbit ear fold

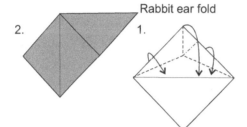

1.

2.

3.

Push the two sides in and fold the corner over.

In progress.

Swivel fold

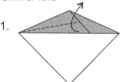

1.

2.

3.

Pull the top layer up.

Continue to pull the layer until it lies flat. Push the area that stands up down.

Open sink

1.

2.

3.

Push the top in and partially open the paper.

Continue to push the top and push the sides in.

Preliminary fold

1.

2.

3.

Squash fold the flap down.

Closed sink

1.

2.

3.

Push the top in while keeping the paper together.

In progress.

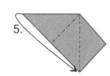

4.

5.

6.

Turn the paper over.

Squash fold the flap down.

HAWKER

Use a square sheet of paper.

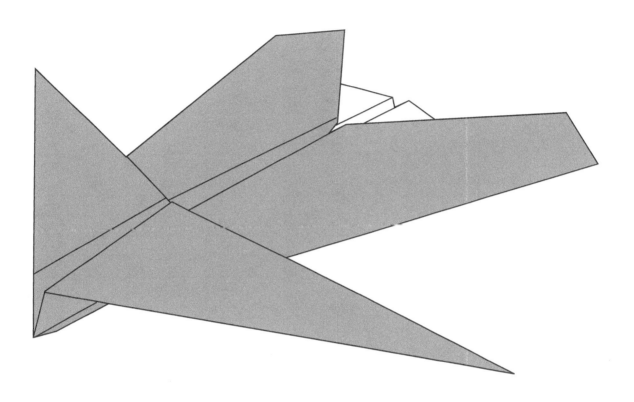

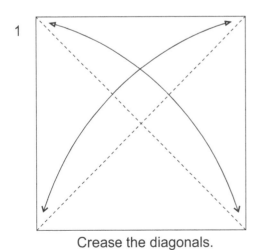

1

Crease the diagonals.

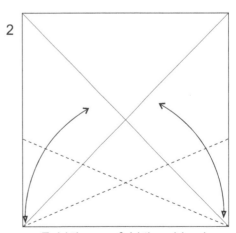

2

Fold then unfold the sides in.

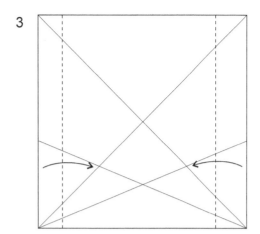

Fold the sides in to the intersections as shown.

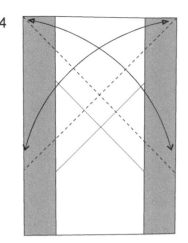

Fold then unfold the sides in.

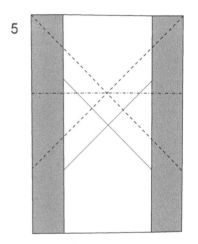

Fold a waterbomb base using the crease you made.

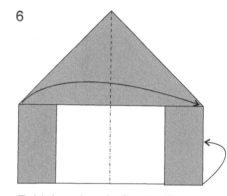

Fold the triangle flap to the top and the rear flap behind.

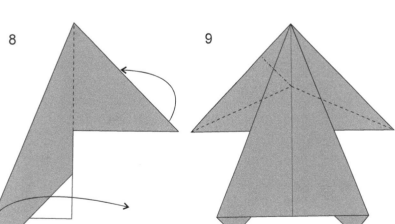

Fold one triangle flap behind and one flap to the front.

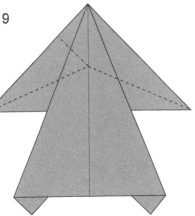

Rabbit ear fold the top flap.

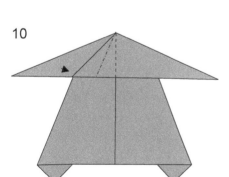

Squash fold the flap over.

11

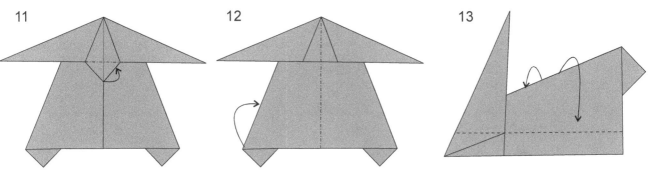

Fold the triangle in.

12

Mountain fold the model in half.

13

Fold the wings down using the intersection shown.

14

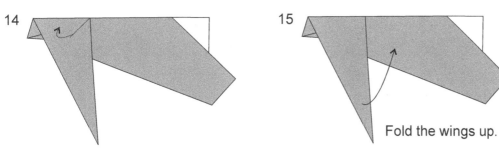

Fold the small portion of the area over to lock the model.

15

Fold the wings up.

16

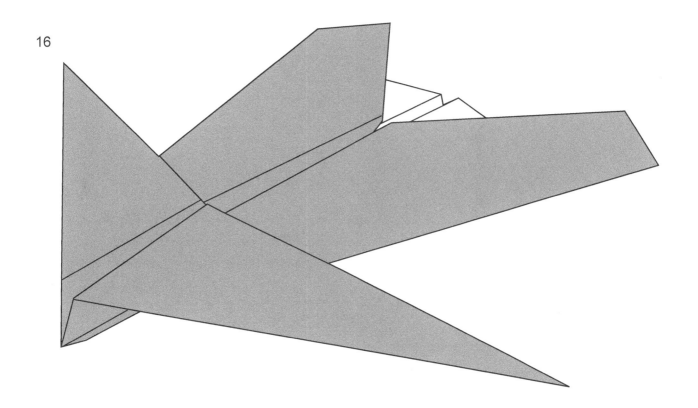

WINGMAN

Use a 6-inch-square sheet of foil paper.

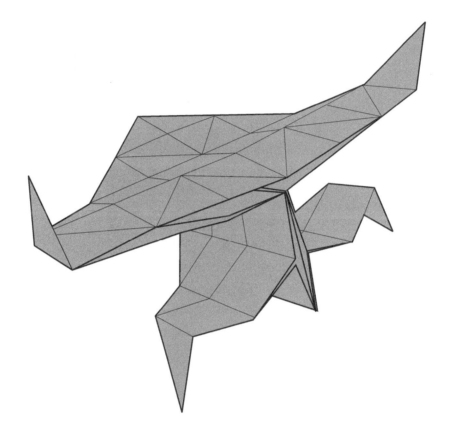

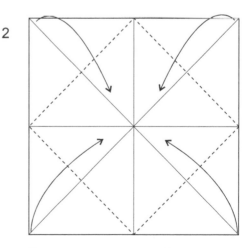

1

Make the creases shown.

2

Fold the corners in to form a blintz base.

3

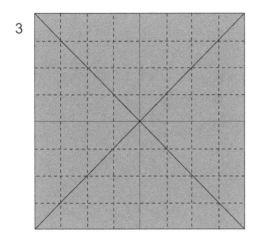

4

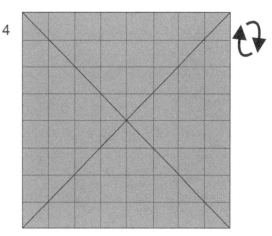

Turn the model over.

5

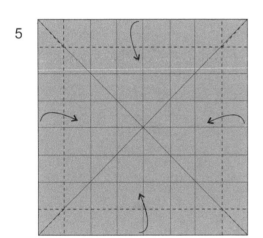

Rabbit ear fold the sides in.

6

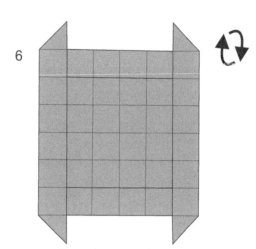

Turn the model over.

7

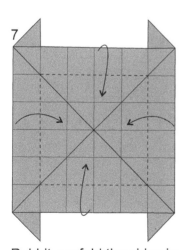

Rabbit ear fold the sides in.

8

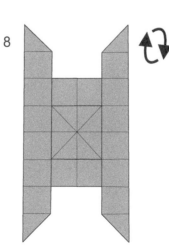

Turn the model over.

9

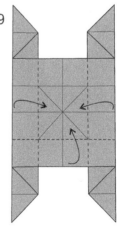

Rabbit ear only the sides and the bottom edge.

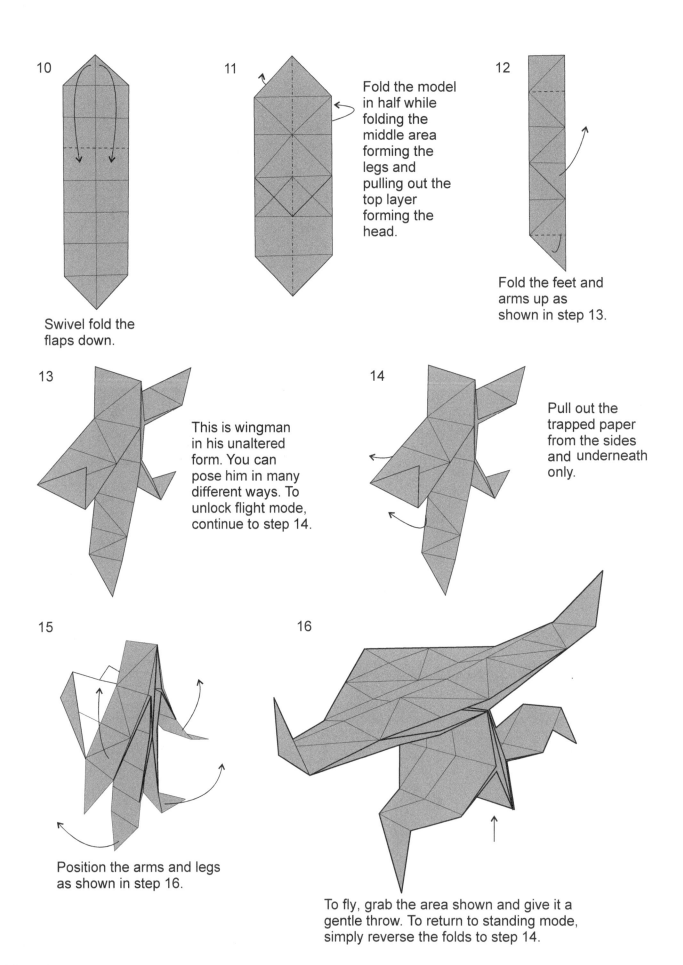

10

Swivel fold the flaps down.

11

Fold the model in half while folding the middle area forming the legs and pulling out the top layer forming the head.

12

Fold the feet and arms up as shown in step 13.

13

This is wingman in his unaltered form. You can pose him in many different ways. To unlock flight mode, continue to step 14.

14

Pull out the trapped paper from the sides and underneath only.

15

Position the arms and legs as shown in step 16.

16

To fly, grab the area shown and give it a gentle throw. To return to standing mode, simply reverse the folds to step 14.

STRATUS

Use a square sheet of paper.

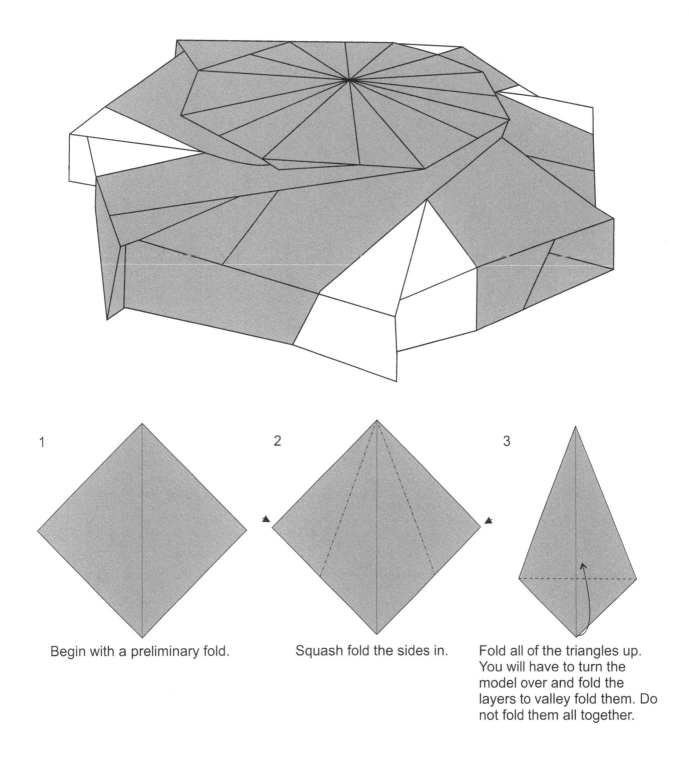

1

Begin with a preliminary fold.

2

Squash fold the sides in.

3

Fold all of the triangles up. You will have to turn the model over and fold the layers to valley fold them. Do not fold them all together.

4

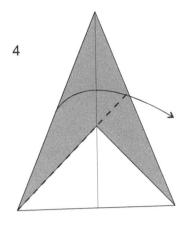

5

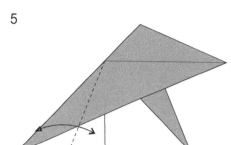

6

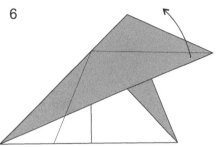

7

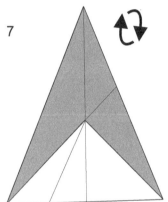

Turn the model over.

8

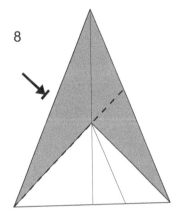

Repeat steps 4-7 to this side.

9

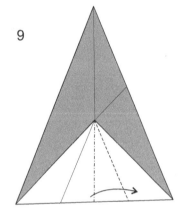

Crimp the paper over using the fold you just made.

10

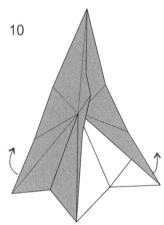

Completely spread the bottom out using this method. Use step 11 as a reference.

11

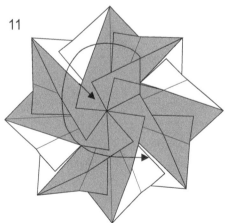

Continue to push the edges in and push down on the center region.

12

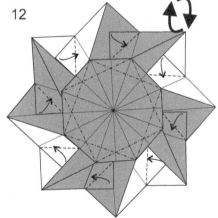

Valley fold the small triangles in. Mountain fold the sides of the center octagon in. Then turn the model over.

13

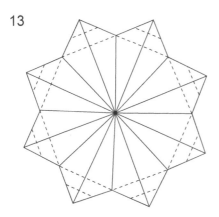

Divide the small triangles in two and roll them in.

14

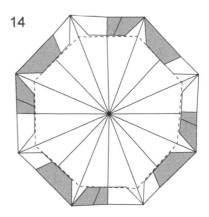

Rabbit ear fold the edges in simultaneously.

15

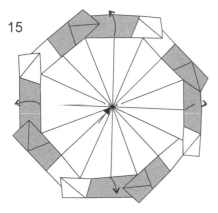

Slightly inflate the center octagon, then stand the sides up. Use step 16 as a reference.

16

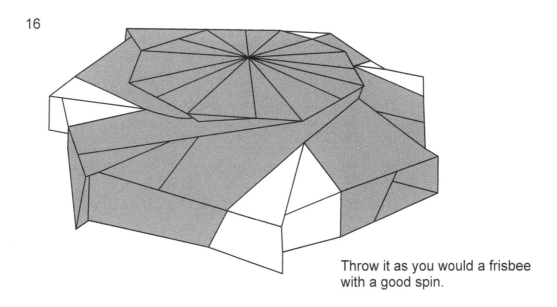

Throw it as you would a frisbee with a good spin.

F-X

Use a square sheet of paper of your choice.

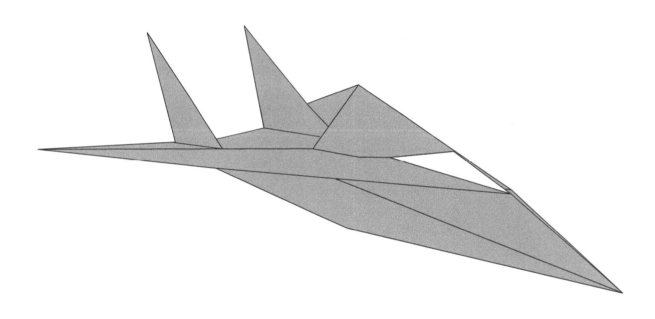

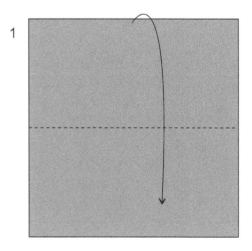

1

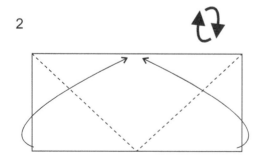

2

Fold the edges in, then turn the model over.

3

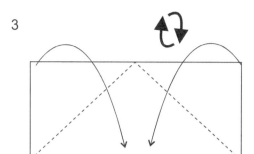

Fold the edges in, then turn the model over.

4

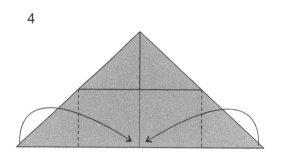

5

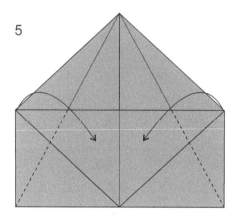

6

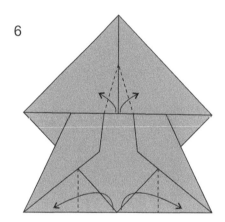

7

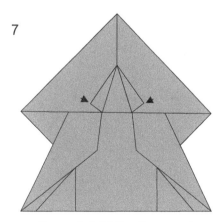

Squash fold the flaps out.

8

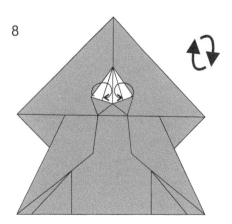

Inside reverse fold only the layers shown, then turn the model over.

9

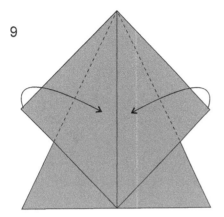

Fold the sides in as shown.

10

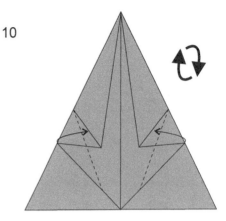

Fold the sides in, then turn the model over.

11

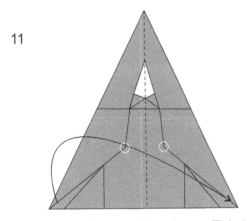

Note the intersection shown. This is what you will use as a guide point for the next step.

12

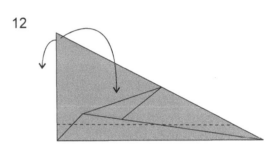

Using the intersection from step 11 as a guide, fold the wings down.

13

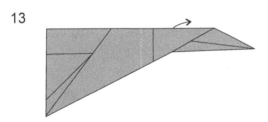

Inside reverse fold the area up inside the nose.

14

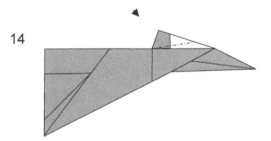

Inside reverse fold the area in as shown.

15

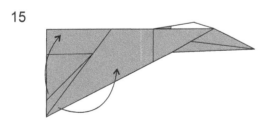

Fold the wings up and fold the tailfins up perpendicular to the wings.

16

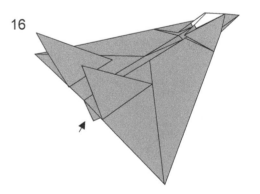

Fold the middle layer up to lock the model.

17

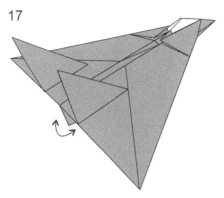

Round the two remaining layers to form an afterburner.

18

AVENGER

Use a square sheet of paper of your choice.

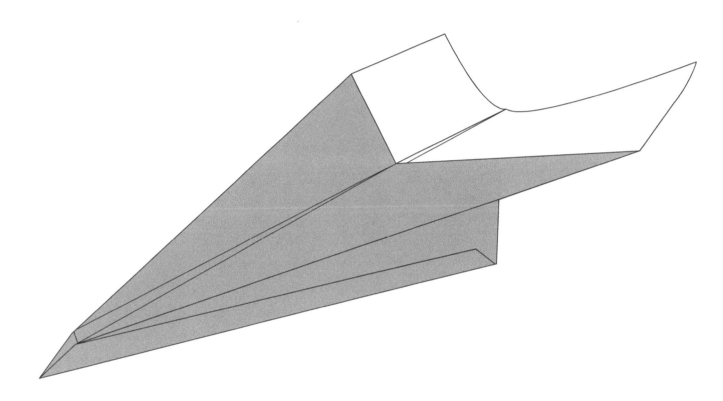

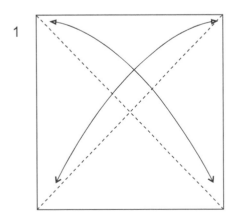

1

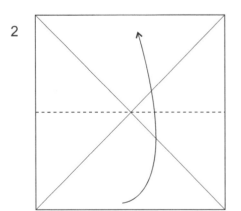

2

3

4

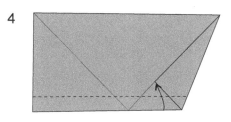

5

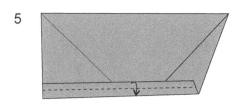

6

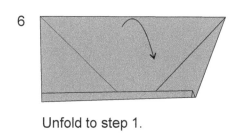

Unfold to step 1.

7

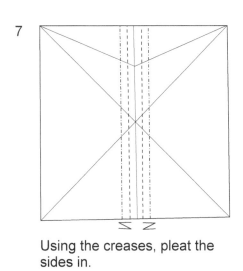

Using the creases, pleat the sides in.

8

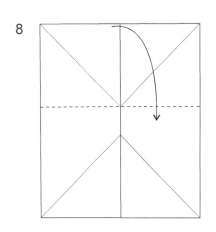

9

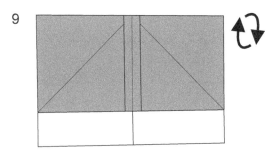

Turn the model over.

10

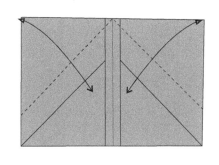

11

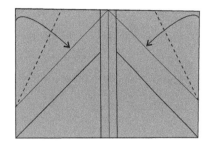

12

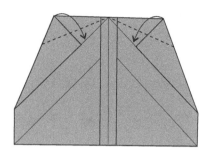

13

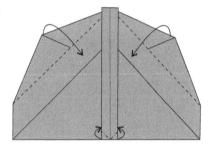

14

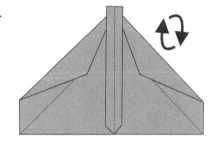

Turn the model over.

15

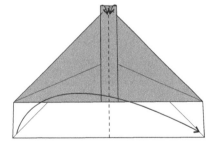

Fold the small triangle in, then fold
the model in half.

16

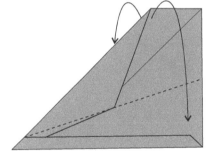

Fold the wings down as shown.

17

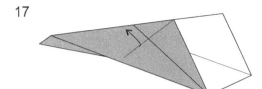

Fold the inner area over to lock the model together.

18

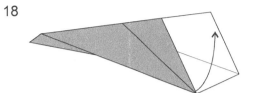

Fold the wings up as shown.

19

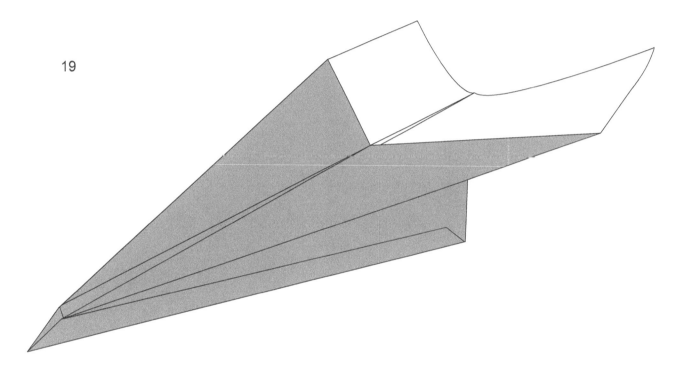

CIRRUS

Use a square sheet of paper of your choice.

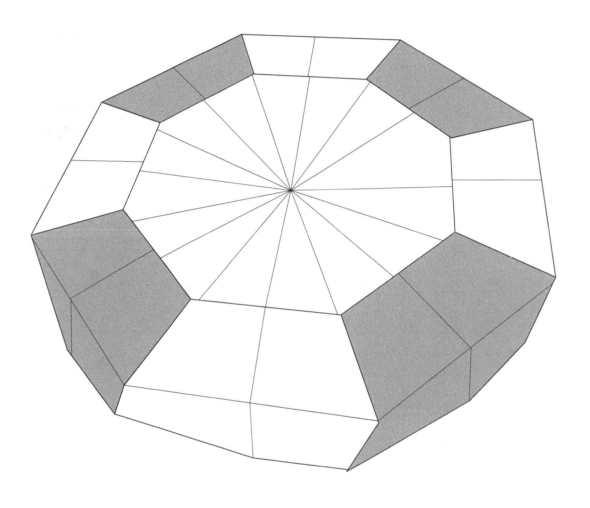

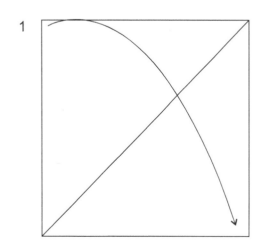

1

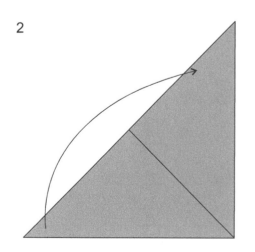

2

3

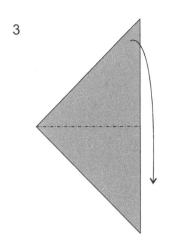

Squash fold the flap down.

4

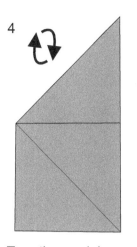

Turn the model over.

5

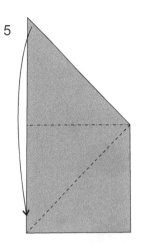

Squash fold the flap down.

6

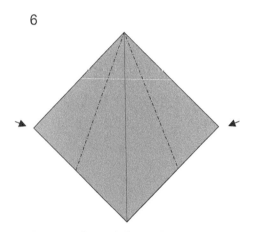

Squash fold all four sides in.

7

Unfold to step 1.

8

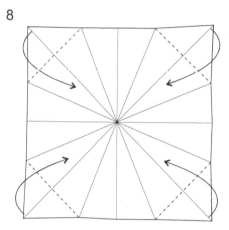

9

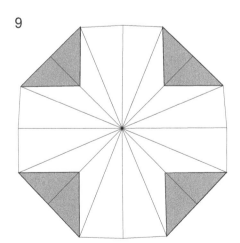

10

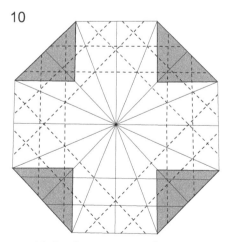

Make the creases shown.

11

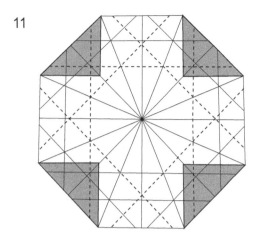

Rabbit ear fold the sides in simultaneously.

12

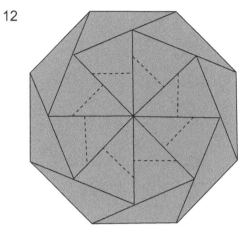

Using the creases made in step 10, simultaneously fold the edges back.

13

Turn the model over.

14

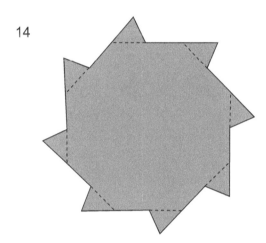

Fold the small triangles in.

15

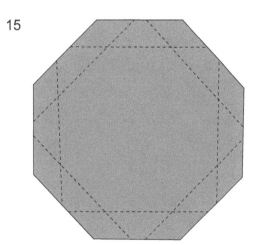

Rabbit ear fold the sides in simultaneously.

16

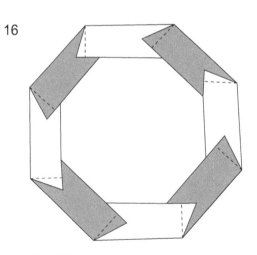

Fold the sides up.

17

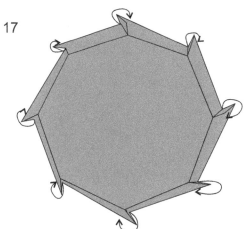

Pull the edges around and tuck
them into the pockets. Then turn
the model over.

18

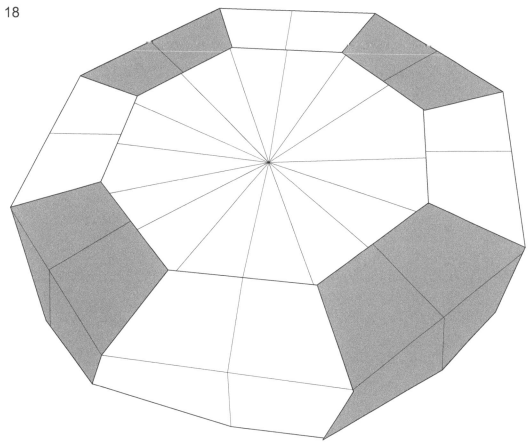

Give this a light throw with some spin.
It will fly slowly and smoothly.

HEX

Use a square sheet of paper of your choice.

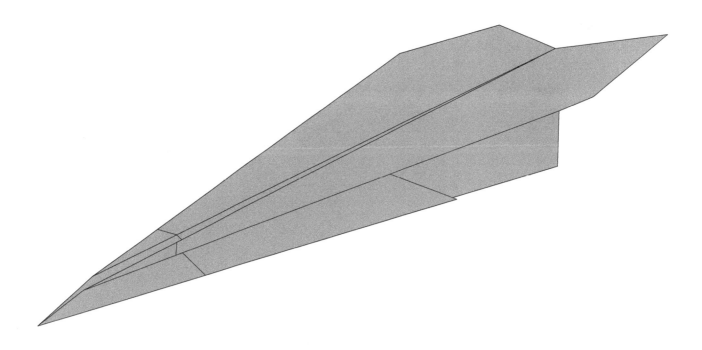

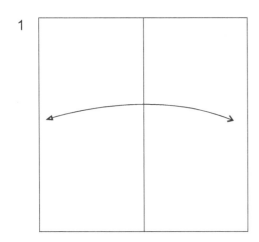

1

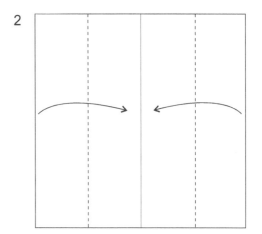

2

3

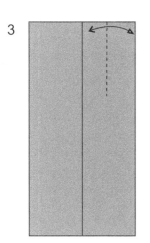

Fold only a small area.

4

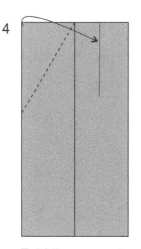

Fold the corner to
the line but do not
cross the center line.

5

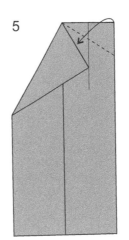

6

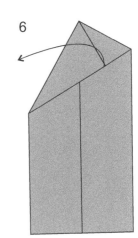

7

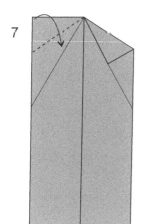

8

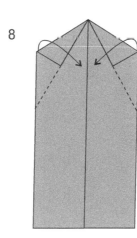

Fold the
sides in
and fold
edges
underneath
the bottom
layers.

9

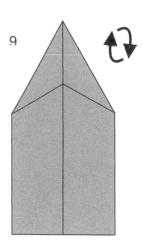

Turn the model over.

10

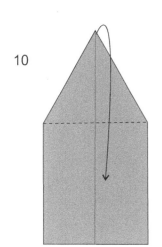

11

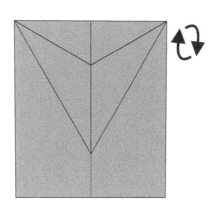

Turn the model over.

12

Repeat steps 3–9.

29

13

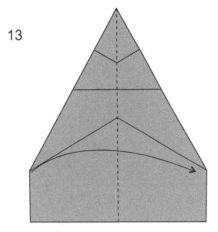

Fold the model in half.

14

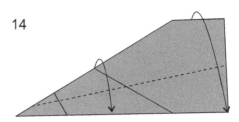

Fold the wings down so that the intersection shown touches the keel and the back edge of the wing touches the corner of the keel.

15

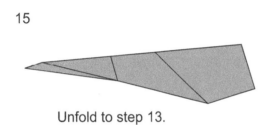

Unfold to step 13.

16

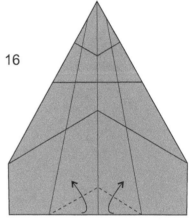

Fold the edges up 1/3 of the angle.

17

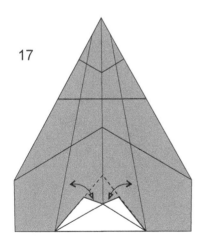

18

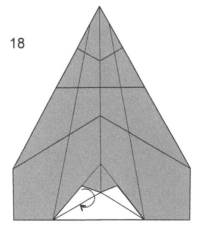

Fold one layer underneath.

19

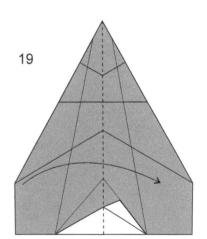

20

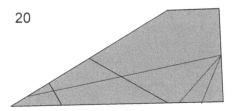

Using the creases you just made, roll the two layers of paper together to lock the model.

21

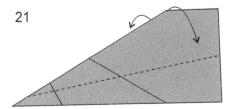

Fold the wings down.

22

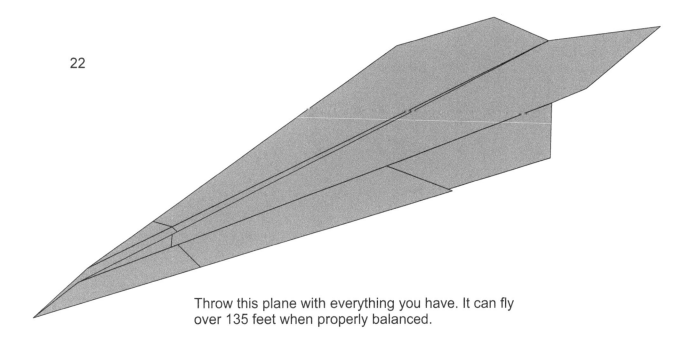

Throw this plane with everything you have. It can fly over 135 feet when properly balanced.

AEON

Use a square sheet of paper of your choice.

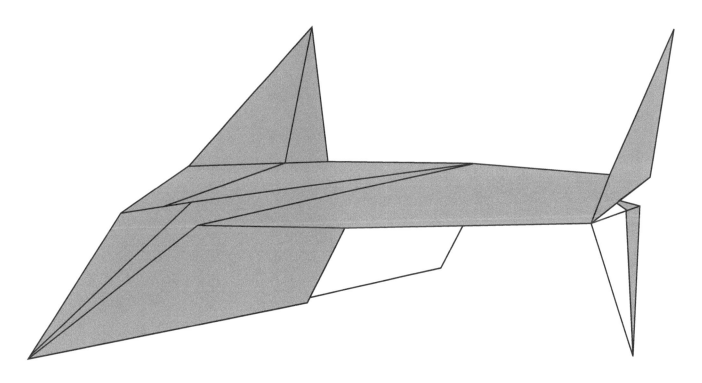

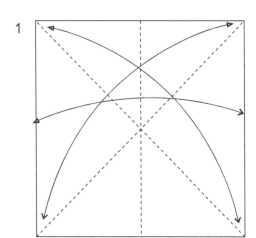

Crease the diagonals and the
center line.

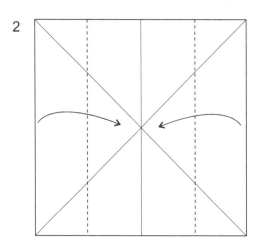

3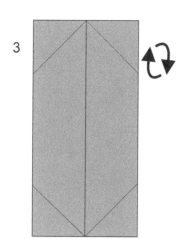

Turn the model over.

4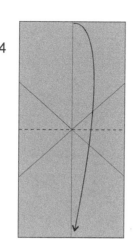

5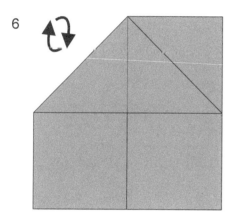

Squash fold the side over.

6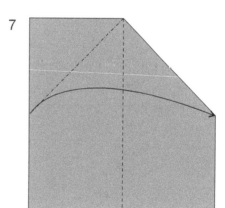

Turn the model over.

7

Squash fold the side over.

8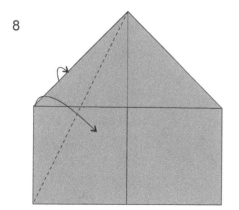

Fold the sides over, repeat behind.

9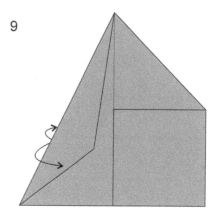

Pull out the layer of paper from inside. Repeat behind.

10

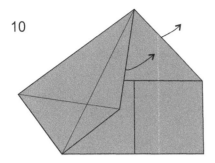

Slide the inner paper over and move the edge out. Repeat behind.

11

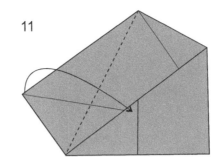

12

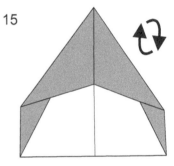

Roll the edge under. Repeat behind.

13

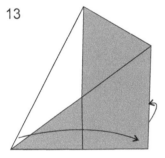

Fold one flap to the front and one to the back.

14

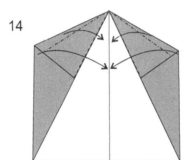

Fold the edges over but slide the excess in so it meets the center line.

15

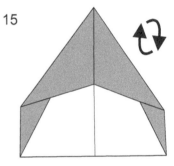

Turn the model over.

16

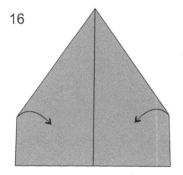

17

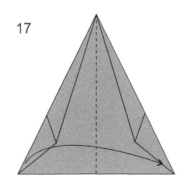

18

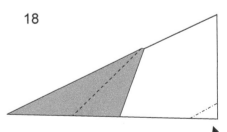

Fold the edge of the triangle in. Inside reverse fold all of the rear layers to one side to lock the model together.

19

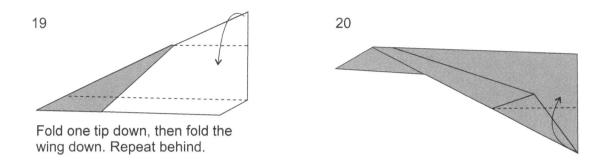

Fold one tip down, then fold the
wing down. Repeat behind.

20

21

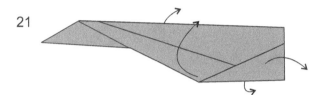

Fold the wings up and the wing tips out.

22

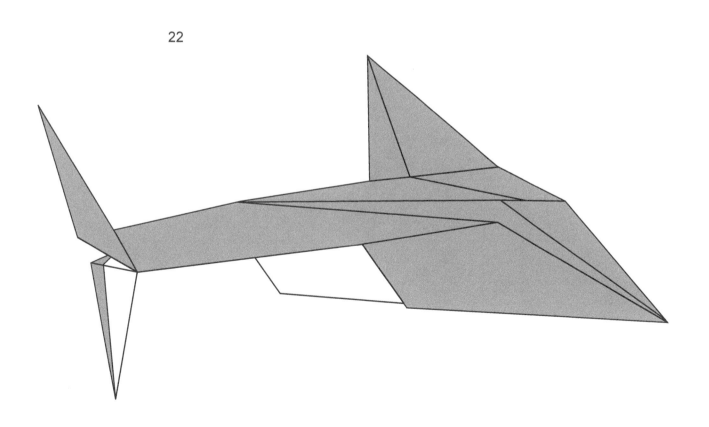

SUNDOWN

Use a square sheet of paper of your choice.

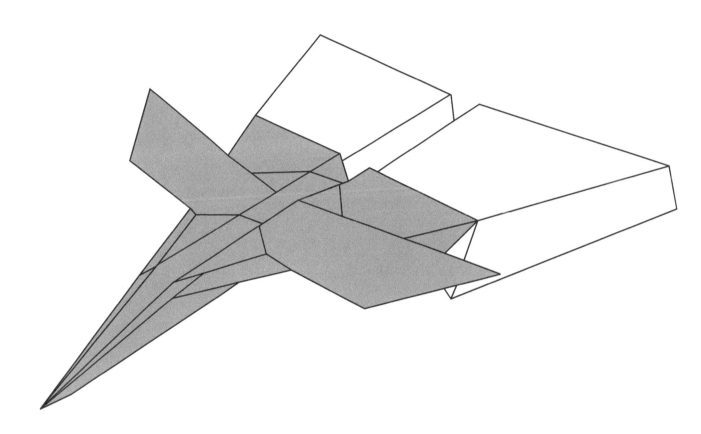

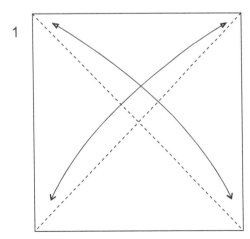

1

Make the creases shown.

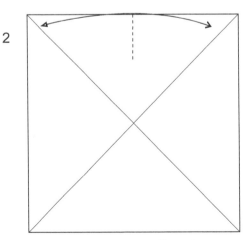

2

Crease only a small part.

3

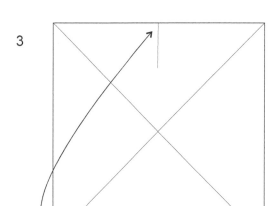

Fold the bottom corner up to the intersection shown.

4

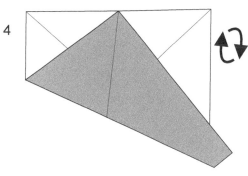

Turn the model over.

5

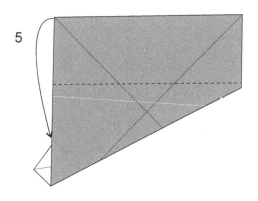

6

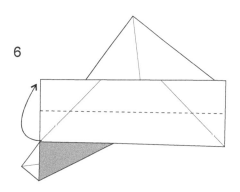

7

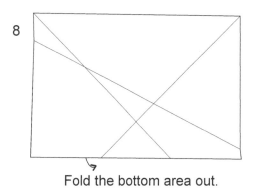

Fold the area down.

8

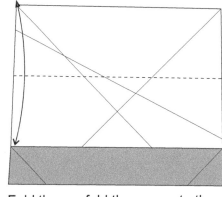

Fold the bottom area out.

9

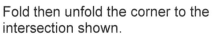

Fold then unfold the corner to the intersection shown.

10

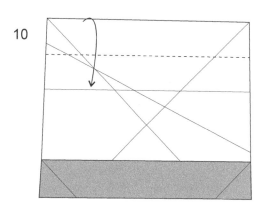

11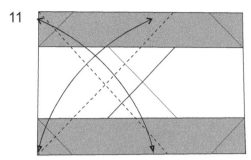

Make the creases shown.

12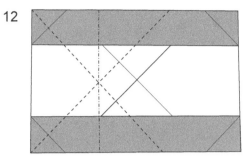

Fold a waterbomb base from the crease you just made.

13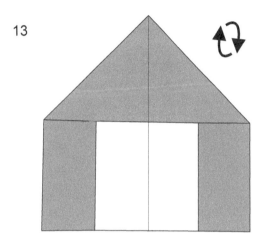

Turn the model over.

14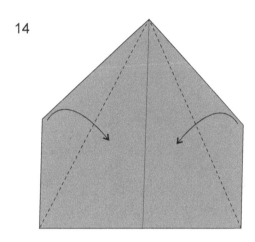

15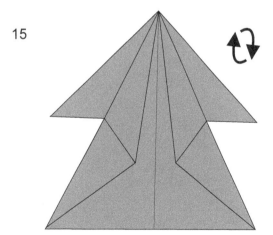

Turn the model over.

16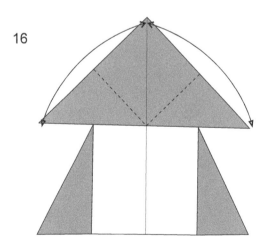

17

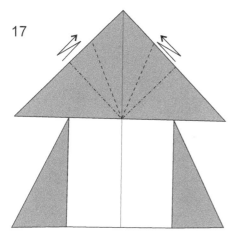

Crimp the sides in as shown.

18

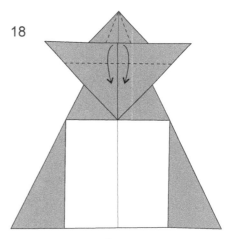

Swivel fold the flaps down.

19

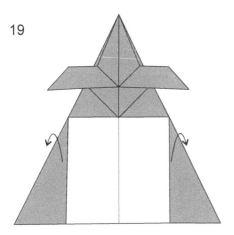

Fold the flaps around.

20

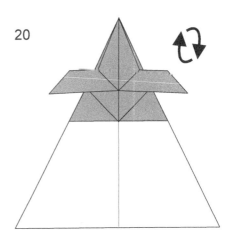

Turn the model over.

21

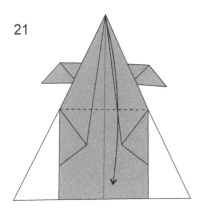

22

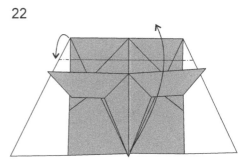

Fold the top edge back and swing the flap up.

23

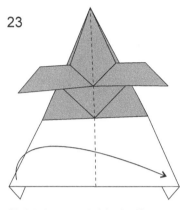

Fold the model in half.

24

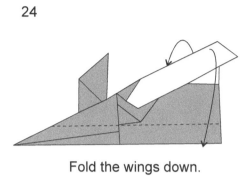

Fold the wings down.

25

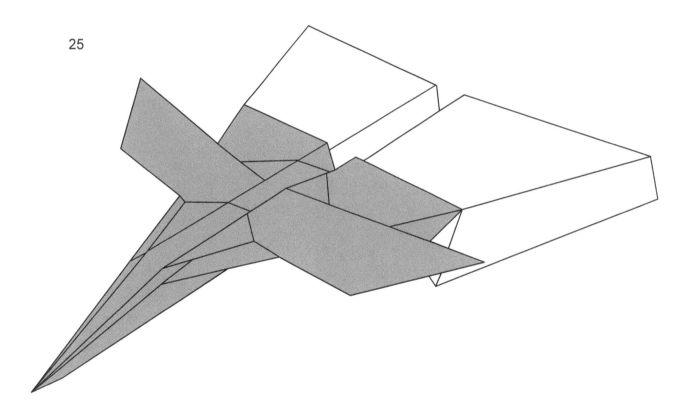

RAZORBACK

Use a square sheet of paper of your choice.

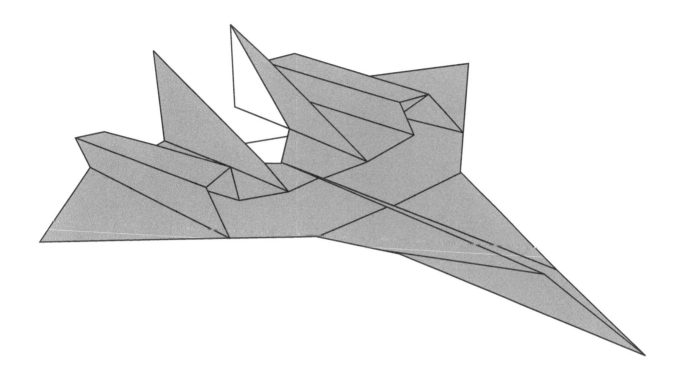

1

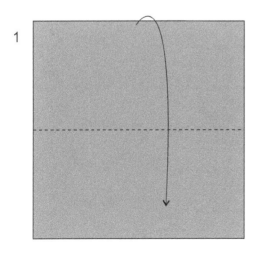

2

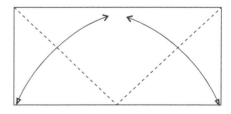

Fold then unfold.

3

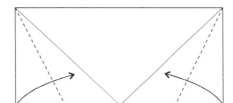

4

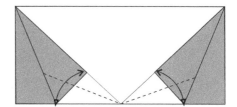

Fold then unfold.

5

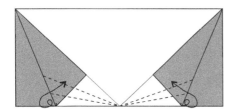

Using the creases, fold the edge over twice.

6

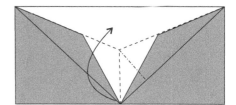

Rabbit ear fold the flap over.

7

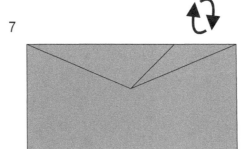

Turn the model over.

8

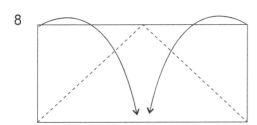

9

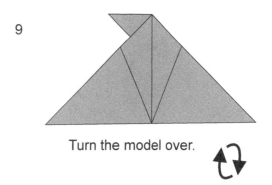

Turn the model over.

10

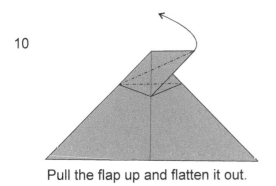

Pull the flap up and flatten it out.

11

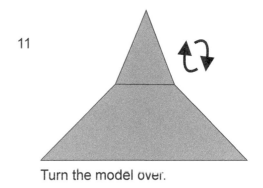

Turn the model over.

12

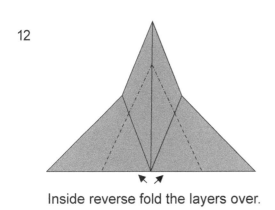

Inside reverse fold the layers over.

13

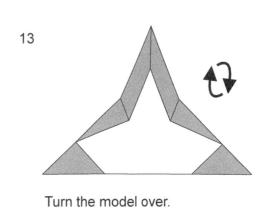

Turn the model over.

14

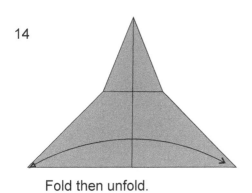

Fold then unfold.

15

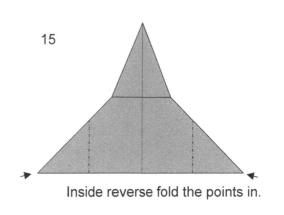

Inside reverse fold the points in.

16

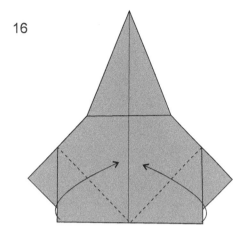

17

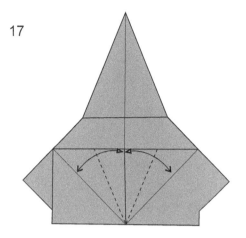

18

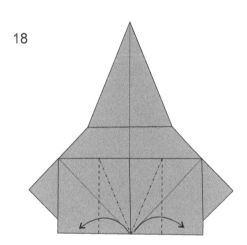

19

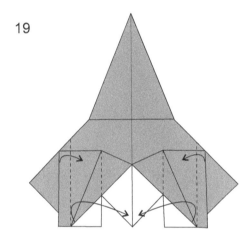

20

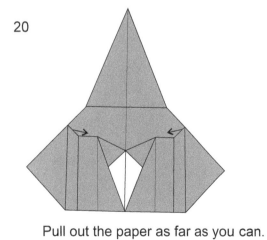

Pull out the paper as far as you can.

21

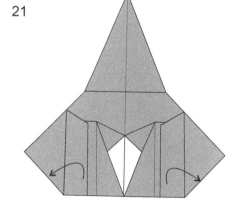

Return the paper to step 18.

22

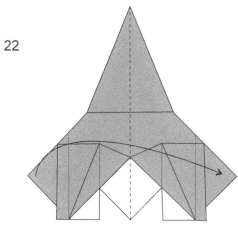

Fold the model in half.

23

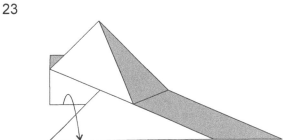

Using the back edges of the wing as a guide, fold it to the bottom of the keel.

24

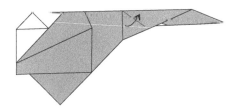

Fold the small triangle over in the middle of the keel to lock the model together.

25

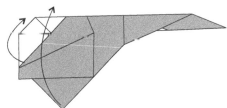

Fold the wings up, fold the tailfins out, and position the engines.

26

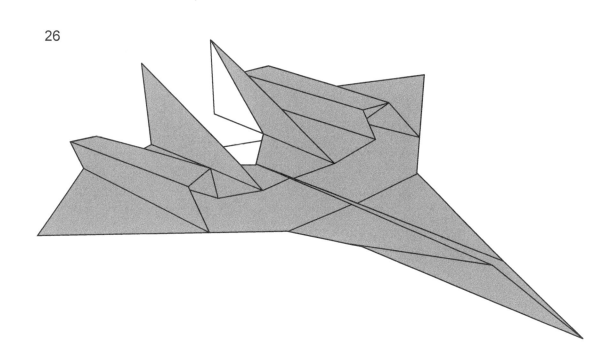

HAMMER

Use a square sheet of paper of your choice.

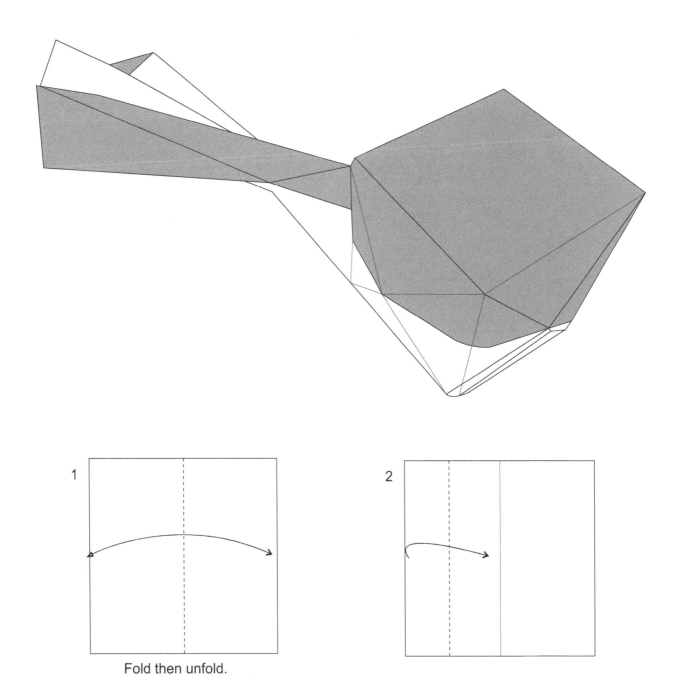

1

Fold then unfold.

2

3

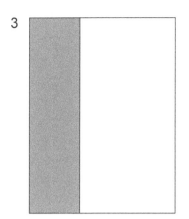

Turn the model over.

4

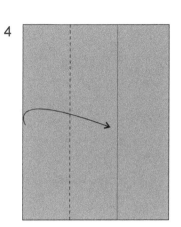

5

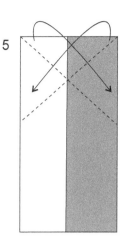

6

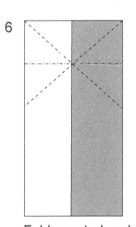

Fold a waterbomb base from the creases you just made.

7

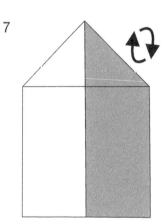

Turn the model over.

8

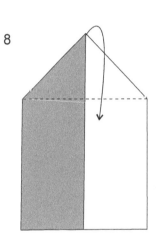

9

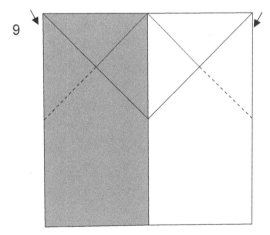

Inside reverse fold the edges in.

10

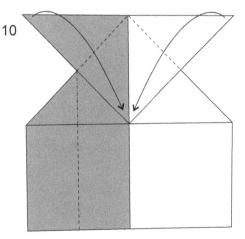

Fold the top flaps down, fold the side in and swivel the small triangle up. This will decrease thickness in a later step.

11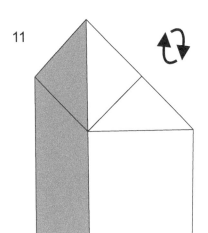

Turn the model over.

12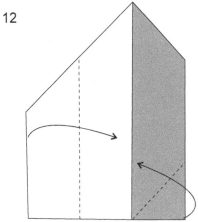

13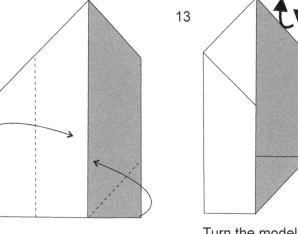

Turn the model over.

14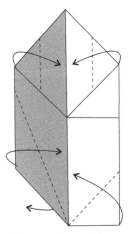

Fold the sides of the waterbomb in. Fold the bottom corner over. Fold the long edge over and allow the flap behind to swing out.

15

16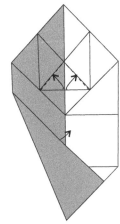

Swivel the paper from underneath out. Fold the small flaps into the pockets.

17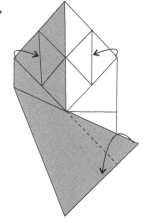

Fold the rear corners in, then lock the waterbomb together.

18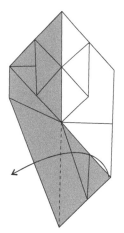

19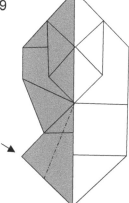

Squash fold the flap out.

20

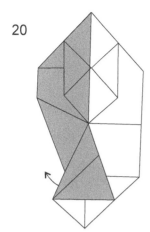

Pull the paper from underneath out.

21

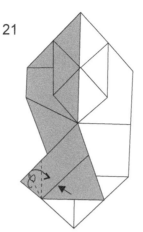

Fold the edge over and tuck it into the small pocket behind.

22

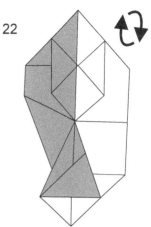

Turn the model over.

23

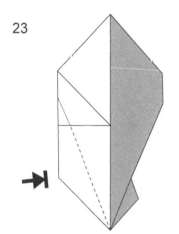

Repeat steps 14–22 to this side.

24

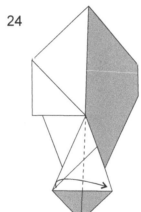
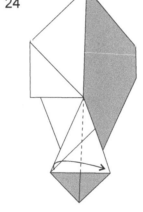

25

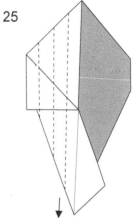

Divide the edge into fourths, then roll it over.

26

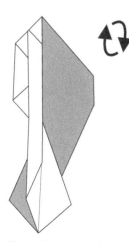

Turn the model over.

27

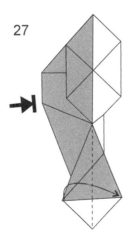

Repeat steps 24–26 to this side.

28

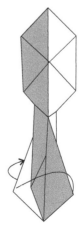

Inflate the waterbomb and fold the fins up. You will also have to slightly reposition the waterbomb.

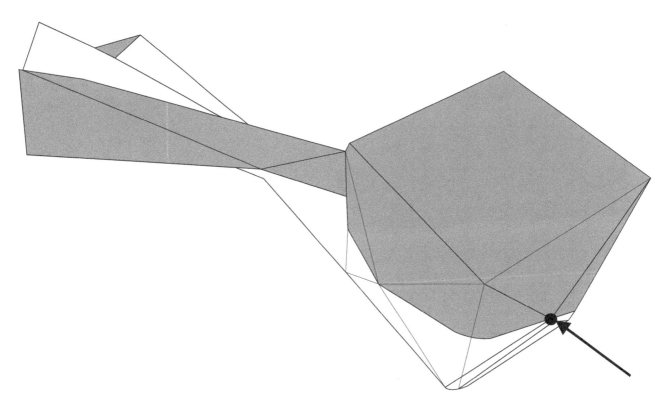

Just like a normal waterbomb, use the hole that you inflated this with to fill it up
with water, ketchup, flour, or whatever you wish and then throw it.

LONGSWORD

Use a 6-inch-square sheet of paper.

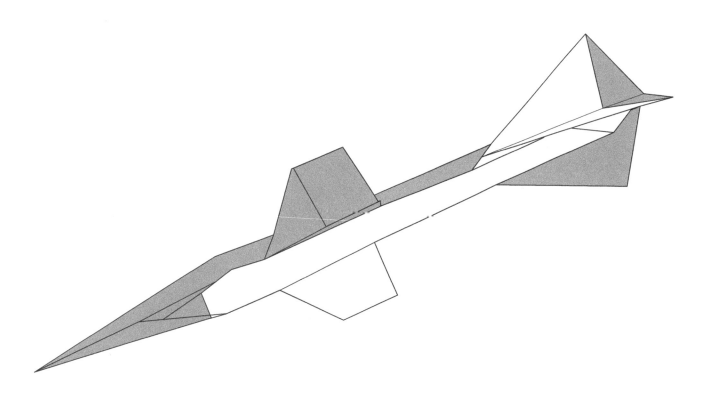

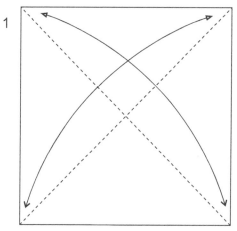

1

Crease the diagonals.

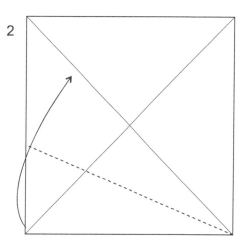

2

3

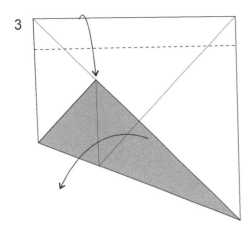

4

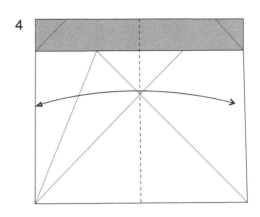

5

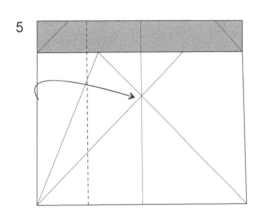

6

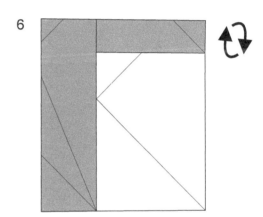

Turn the model over.

7

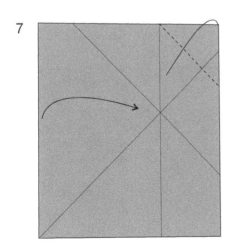

8

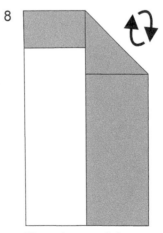

Turn the model over.

9

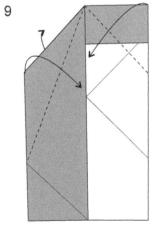

Fold the left side in
and let the flap behind
swing around.

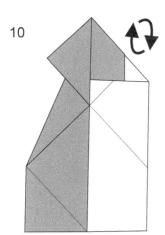

10

Turn the model over.

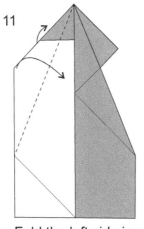

11

Fold the left side in and let the flap behind swing around.

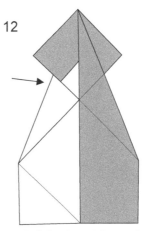

12

Unfold the side and inside reverse fold it along the creases you just made.

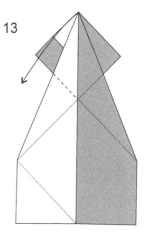

13

Fold the flap down.

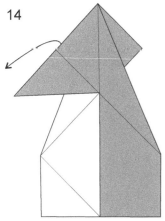

14

Pull the paper from underneath out.

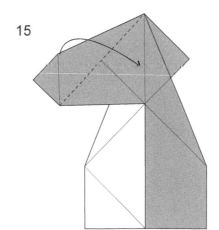

15

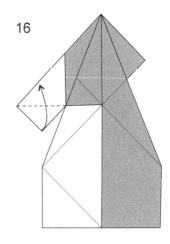

16

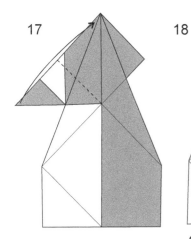

17

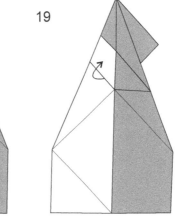

18

Swivel fold the flap down.

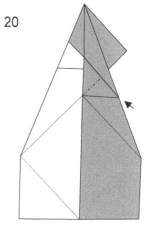

19

Pull the corner from underneath out.

20

Squash fold this flap.

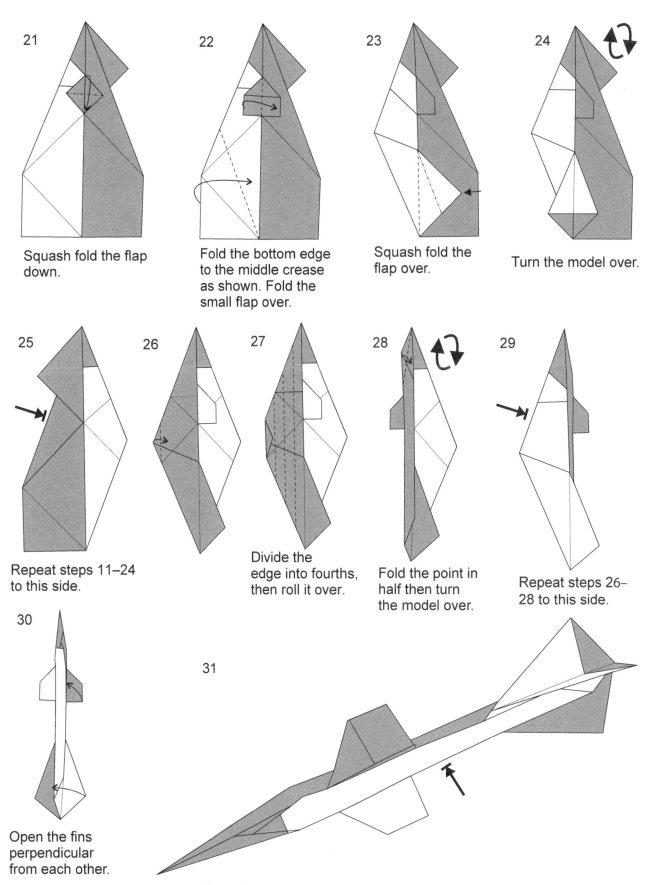

21 Squash fold the flap down.

22 Fold the bottom edge to the middle crease as shown. Fold the small flap over.

23 Squash fold the flap over.

24 Turn the model over.

25 Repeat steps 11–24 to this side.

26

27 Divide the edge into fourths, then roll it over.

28 Fold the point in half then turn the model over.

29 Repeat steps 26–28 to this side.

30 Open the fins perpendicular from each other.

31 Grab the area shown and throw it with all of your strength.

DARK KNIGHT

Use a square sheet of paper of your choice.

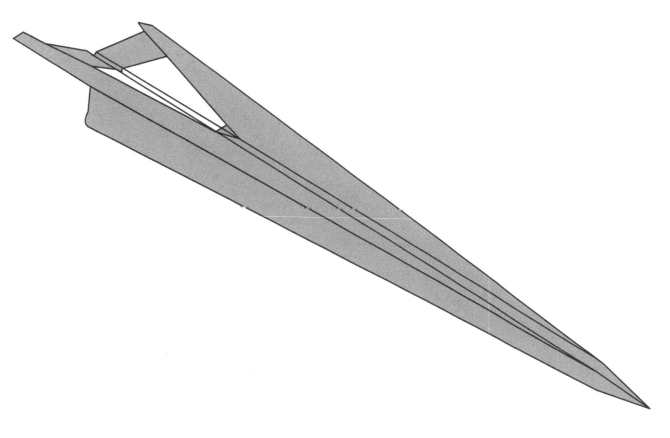

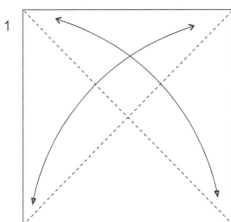

Crease the diagonals.

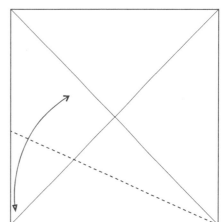

3

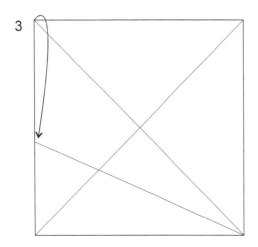

4

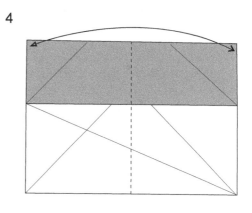

5

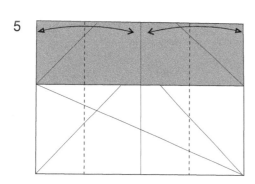

6

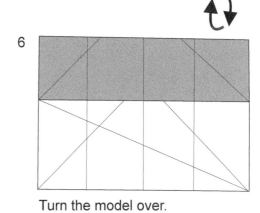

Turn the model over.

7

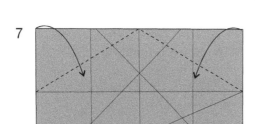

8

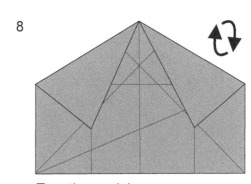

Turn the model over.

9

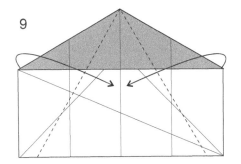

10

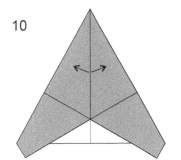

Pull the paper from
underneath out.

11

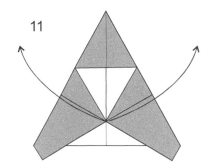

Pull the inner corners
out as shown.

12

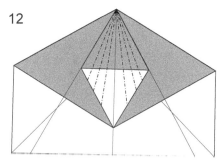

Roll the edge into fourths and
fold it underneath.

13

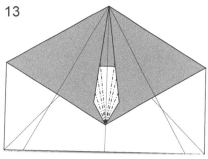

Roll the edge into fourths and
fold it underneath.

14

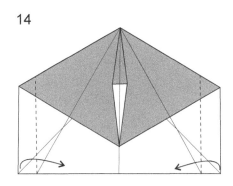

15

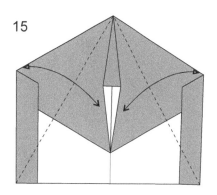

16

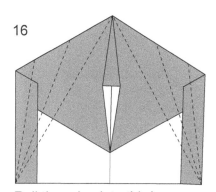

Roll the edge into thirds.

17

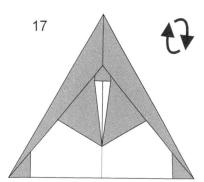

Turn the model over.

18

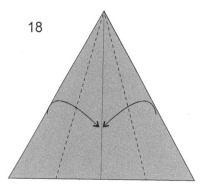

Fold the sides in.

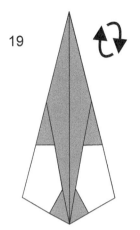

19

Turn the model over.

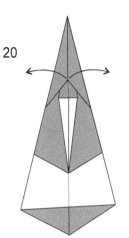

20

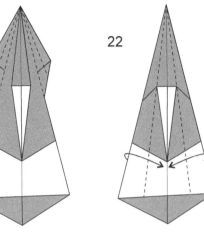

21

Roll the edge over.

22

Fold the sides in and swing the back edges out.

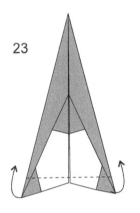

23

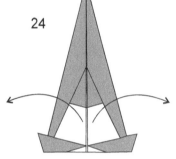

24

Unfold the wings as shown in step 25.

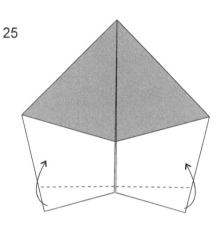

25

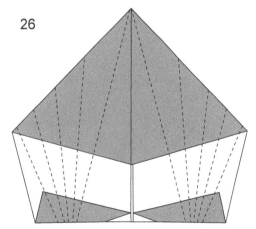

26

Using the creases, roll the wings back to their original position.

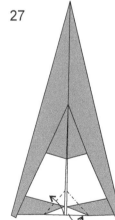

27

Fold one edge up and one edge in. Then unfold them. Note the small white triangles. You will have to insert the other tab into them to lock the model together.

28

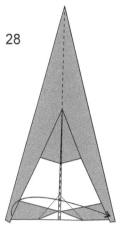

Fold the model in half.

29

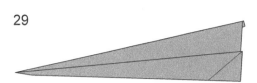

Place one edge into the other,
then fold them up together.

30

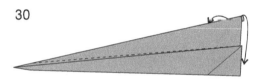

Fold the wings down as shown.

31

You will need to round the bottom edge.
This will help stabilize the model. When
balancing the model, you will need to very
gently touch the sides shown. You can also
turn up the rear edges of the wings slightly.

32

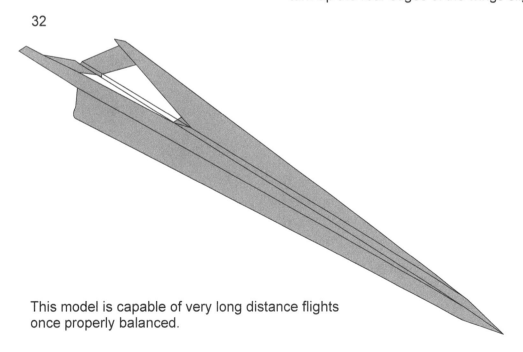

This model is capable of very long distance flights
once properly balanced.

MOURNINGSTAR

Use a 3-inch to 8½-inch square sheet of paper.

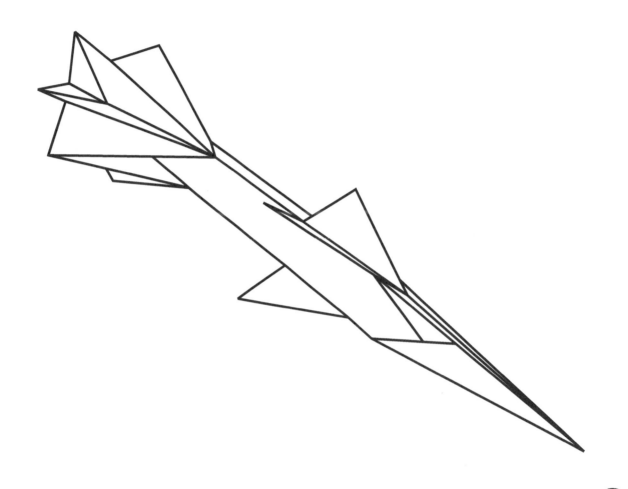

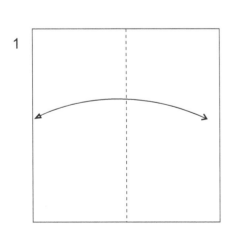

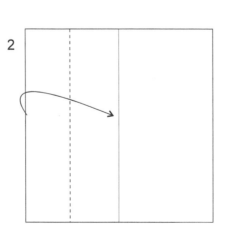

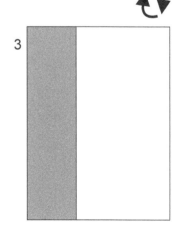

Turn the model over.

4

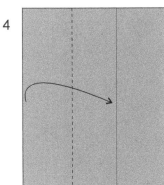

5

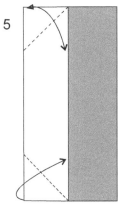

Fold then unfold the
top corner. Fold the
bottom corner over.

6

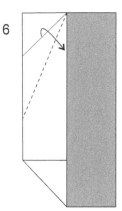

Fold the top edge
into the middle line.

7

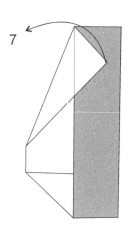

8

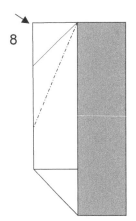

Using the crease you just
made, inside reverse
fold the edge in.

9

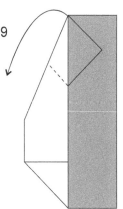

Swivel fold the flap all
the way down.

10

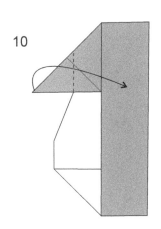

11

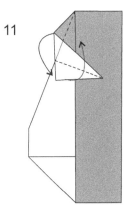

Swivel fold the top
layer down and
simultaneously swivel
fold the bottom layer up.

12

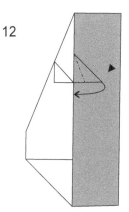

Inside reverse fold
the flap in half.

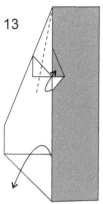

13 Fold then unfold the point in half. Inside reverse fold the small flap in. Fold the bottom corner down.

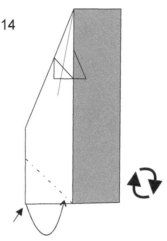

14 Inside reverse fold the bottom corner in, then turn the paper over.

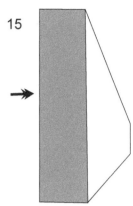

15 Repeat steps 3–14 on this side.

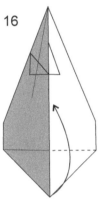

16 Inside reverse fold the bottom flap up.

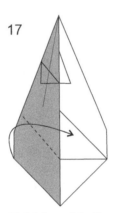

17 Fold the side flap over.

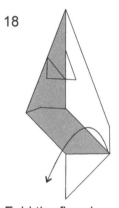

18 Fold the flap down.

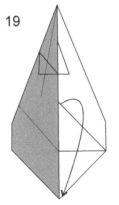

19 Unfold the flaps to step 15.

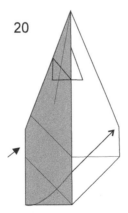

20 Using the crease you made in step 17, inside reverse fold the area over.

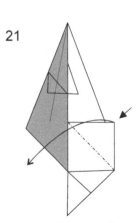

21 Squash fold the flap over.

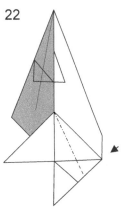

22

Squash fold the flap in.

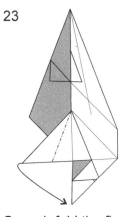

23

Squash fold the flap over.

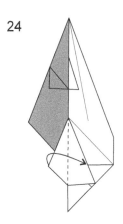

24

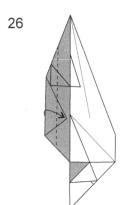

25

Fold the edge in slightly away from the center line.

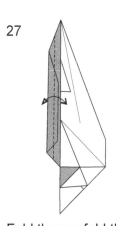

26

27

Fold then unfold the side, then turn the model over.

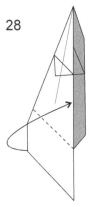

28

Fold the flap over. Note the model will not lie flat.

29

Fold the area over and flatten it out. Use step 30 as a reference.

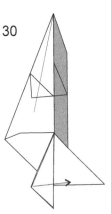

30

Pull the trapped paper from underneath out.

31

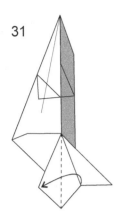

32

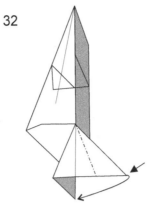

Inside reverse fold the flap in.

33

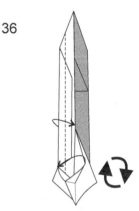

34

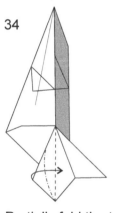

Partially fold the top layer over. Note the paper will not lie flat.

35

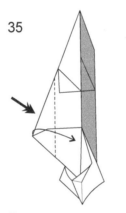

Repeat steps 25–26 on this side.

36

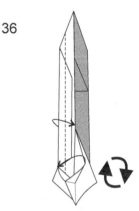

First fold the side in. Then fold the tail back down. Turn the model over.

37

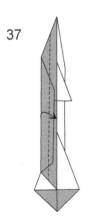

38

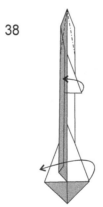

Narrow the tip, fold the front fins perpendicular to each other. Then fold the seven tailfins out evenly.

39

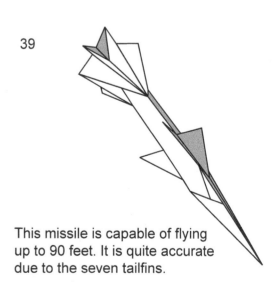

This missile is capable of flying up to 90 feet. It is quite accurate due to the seven tailfins.